THE KNIT-KNOTS

STORY OF
CREATION

To: _____

From: _____

THE KNIT-KNOTS

STORY OF
CREATION

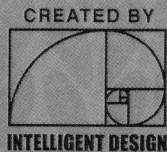

CREATED BY

INTELLIGENT DESIGN

ISBN: 979-8280466241

Published by
Created by Intelligent Design, Nashville, Tennessee
www.theknitknots.com

Text and art copyright © 2025 by Georgina Chidlow-Irvin
Bryan Irvin, Editor

Printed and bound in U.S.A

In the beginning was the WORD.

WHO WAS THE WORD?
The WORD was GOD.

The **WORD** created

HEAVEN

and EARTH

And the WORD said, "Let there be LIGHT!" And there was light.

The **WORD** created light and separated it from darkness.

He called this **DAY** and **NIGHT**.

On the second day, the **WORD** separated the waters in the sky from waters on the earth.

This became
CLOUDS and **OCEANS.**

WHO WAS THE WORD?

The WORD was GOD.

On the third day, the **WORD** created dry land.

PLANTS and TREES grew!

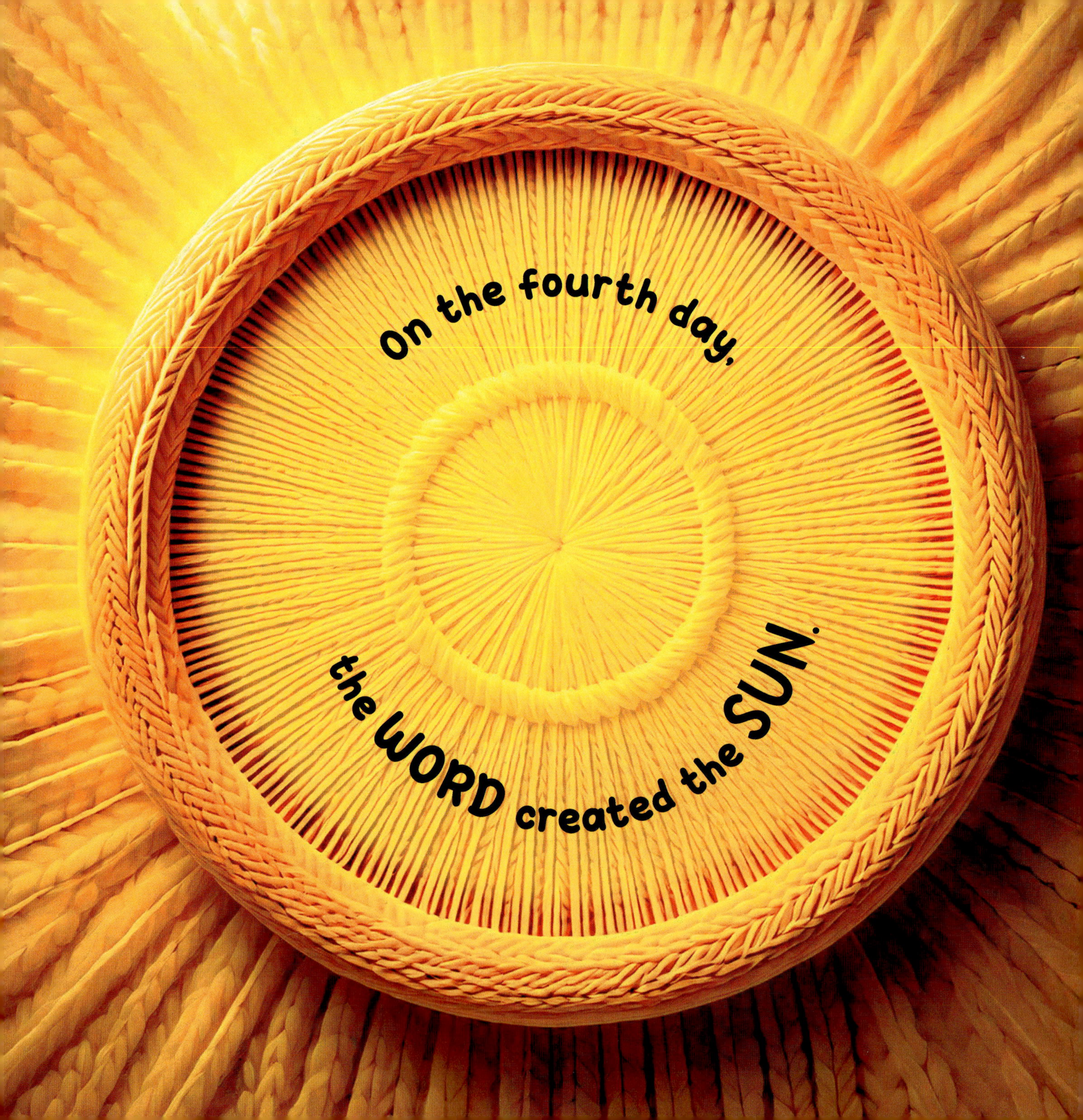

On the fourth day,

the **WORD** created the **SUN**.

And that night He made the STARS sparkle,

and the MOON to shine.

On the fifth day,
the WORD filled the sky with BIRDS,

and the seas with **FISH** and other fantastic sea creatures.

WHO WAS THE WORD?

The **WORD** was **GOD**.

On the sixth day, the
WORD created ANIMALS,

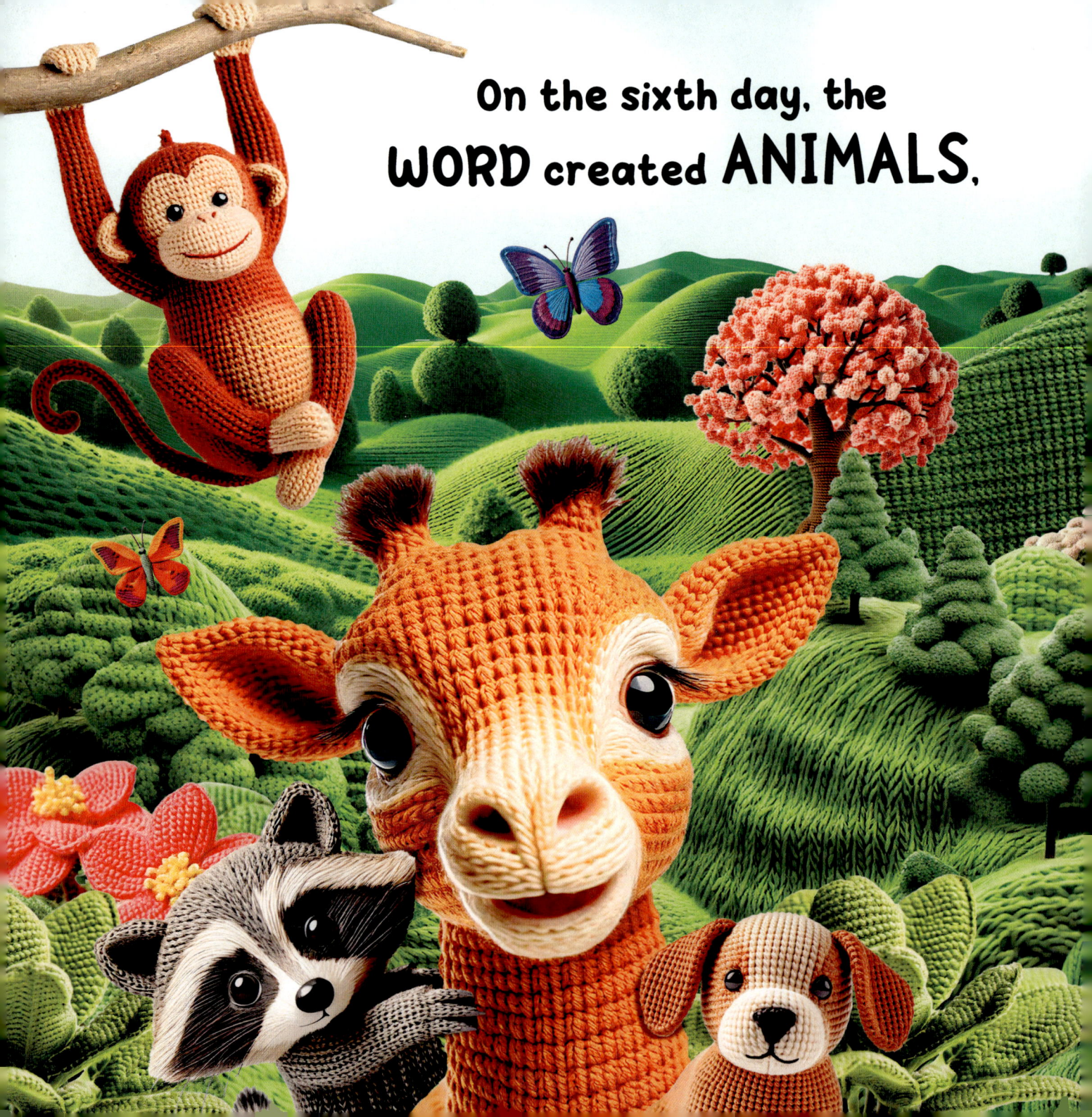

both great and small.

Last, the **WORD** created
ADAM

and then
EVE.

The **WORD** saw all that
He had made, and it
was very good.

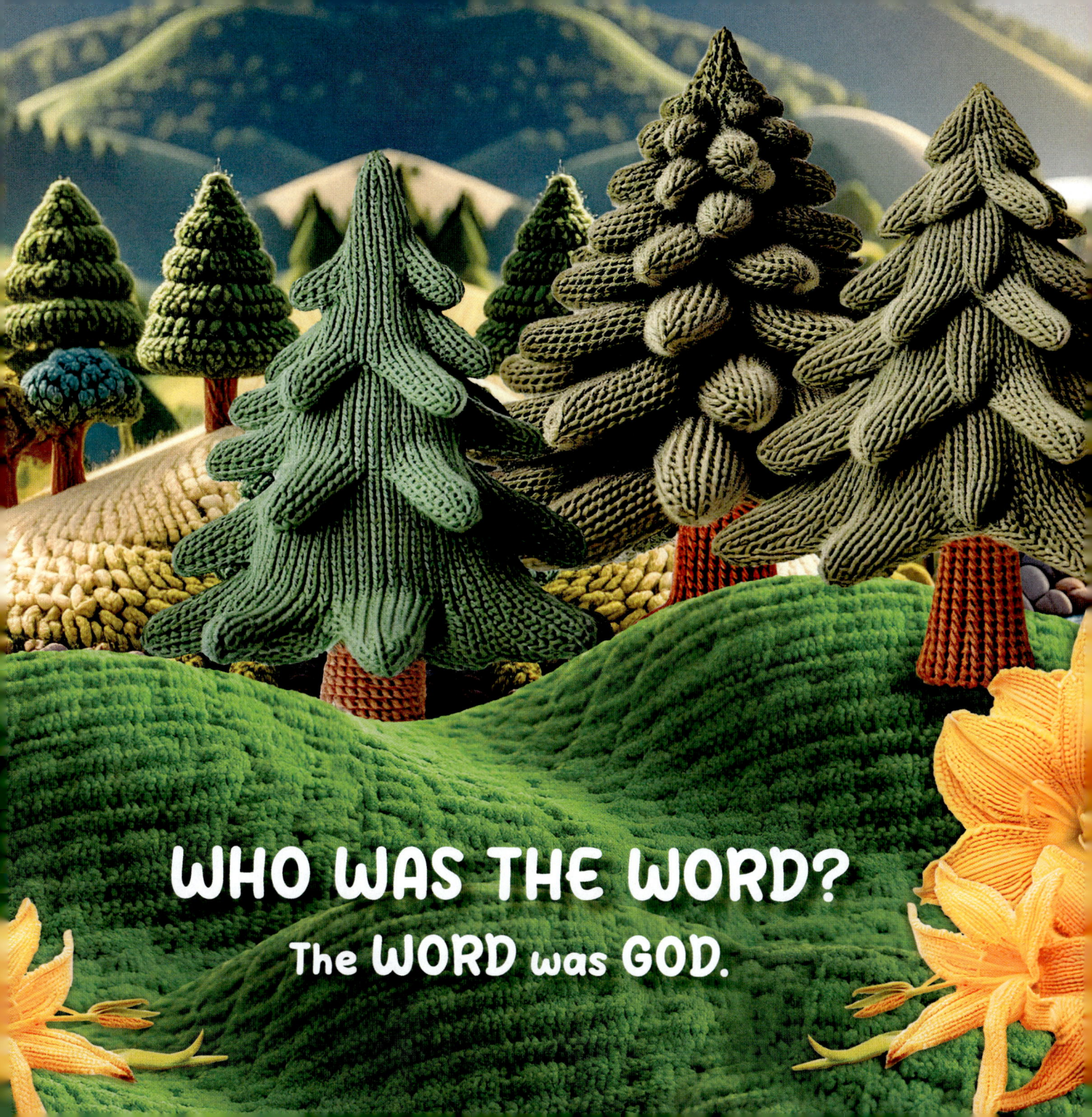

WHO WAS THE WORD?
The WORD was GOD.

On the seventh day,
the **WORD** rested.

Many years later, the **WORD**
became one of us.

WHO WAS THE WORD?
The WORD was JESUS!

"All things were made by him [Jesus]; and without him was not any thing made that was made."
—JOHN 1:3

Made in United States
Orlando, FL
05 July 2025